ALL
THAT'S LEFT
UNSAID

Sana Hamdan

BALBOA.
PRESS

A DIVISION OF HAY HOUSE

Balboa Press books may be ordered through booksellers or by contacting:

Balboa Press
A Division of Hay House
1663 Liberty Drive
Bloomington, IN 47403
www.balboapress.com.au
1 (877) 407-4847

Print information available on the last page.

ISBN: 978-1-5043-0359-0 (sc)
ISBN: 978-1-5043-0360-6 (e)

Balboa Press rev. date: 08/08/2016

CONTENTS

HE WILL ONLY KNOW

These words I've printed between the lines are terms
you will only understand. Each and every love poem I've
written are all about you. Everybody else who have read
my poetry are strangers walking by, witnessing two lovers
among the world's population ignite.

The other day I was speaking about the night sky's aurora
to the sun as it dipped itself within the oceans tides.
I was rambling about how the radiating light had me
dancing to the beat of your heart as your eyes exposed the
constellation of the Galaxy.

The ink coursing within my veins have found their
way to the one thousand and one pages of a book I will
never publish. I adore you through the words I spill, the
limericks I sing and the cuts I bleed from the pages I turn.

INK SPILLING

Most of the time I hate that my writing reveals a little too much, allowing others to stare into my deepest wounds. I feel somewhat bare or exposed. But do tell me what other alternative is better to bleed from than the ink within my pen.

I AM A WRITER

I write to release the inevitable chaos within my broken soul.
To free myself from the burden and sorrow my heart bleeds.
To mask myself with the help of vivid metaphors and
lyrical rhymes,
yet expose the truth as we all read poems differently.
I write because I admire the way my hands freely glide
across the page,
spilling the words my lips refuse to speak.

BETWEEN THESE PAGES

You see the poetry us writers spill, aren't words free of charge.

We all must pay a penalty.

So don't ever think its lies that you read upon these pages.

WHAT IS POETRY?

At the very beginning of discovering poetry,
I realized what its purpose was all about.
Poetry is not the limerick rhymes or hyperboles of life.
Poetry isn't about the sophisticated words of choice made
by the poet.
Poetry is not the production of an educated person.
Poetry is the salvation of poets all over the world.
As writers, we've been baptized within the pure black ink.
The blood our hearts consume, bleed every word we produce.
Poetry is the chaos nested with our minds as they
make their way onto the paper we present.
Poetry is the majestic exploration of one's soul without
meeting them face to face.

ANTIDOTE

"What is it about writing you admire?" He asked curiously.

There was a sudden pause before I responded:

"Writing has become my eternal medicine. The words that I've produced have turned into the antidote for the malicious times that I've lived in."

BURDENS OF THE UNSAID

It's the unsaid thoughts nested within my mind that haunt
me at night.
They're the taunting words I will never speak aloud.
They lured my mind and deprived my heart.
They've kept me in hell for a while now.

PERSONIFICATION

I wonder what it would be like to face the personification of my soul. Staring at its flaws, embracing each scar left on something precious. Spending my nights listening to it ramble about what a tough day it's been.

What if I met the personification of my heart? Broken and empty, yet so full of life. I would be cautious with the words I say because I know how sensitive and fragile it can be at times.

What about my diary's personification. I really wouldn't know if I could have the guts to spill as much as I write in it these days. I wonder if the one person could live or keep such mayhem within themselves without spilling any secrets.

But I do know one thing; I would thank all three for supporting me. Through all the traumatic events I have experienced; for those lonely panic attacks and in times where I was alone in misery, they were there.

GLORIOUS POETRY

When I first discovered poetry, my words at first battled against the voices inside of my head. The words that hung on the roof of my mouth made their way onto the page I placed in front of me. I began writing endlessly, through my days and nights. It had felt as if the ink my pen released, eliminated the torturing pain my chest once held. Each word I printed was another knot being untied.

Poetry has given me and other writers a voice to express the mayhem thoughts the mind consumes. Granted a life full of new opportunities. Poetry was once known to me as my lifeline. However, I feel as if it has become more of my life companion. There to remind me on days like today, how far I've grown. Poetry has altered the way I view the world. I no longer capture the flaws of scars and broken hearts. It's the breathtaking view of thousands of daisies glowing on a place that was once full of tragedy.

UNTITLED

Within the realm of my veins a late night blizzard blows
heavily, setting my thoughts numb. Most of the time
I sew the sentences I wish to say, though I don't. As it
appears my tongue has been anchored to the earth's core,
restraining me from speaking another word. The guttural
screams of my demons are getting louder every night,
demanding to be released as they push themselves to the
brink of my pale skin. It isn't long till the black ink of my
pen finds its way to the page.

Silence at last.

DEAREST POETRY

If poetry were a living being, I would hold them so close and whisper;

"O poetry, there are a billion of ways to bleed though you are so far my dearest."

NO POETRY TODAY

The poet is out today as she feels too sick to compose a piece.
It seems the ink coursing through her veins has been
infected by the insults of others.
The words they carelessly spill have found their way into
her body,
gnawing at her dilapidated bones.

When will she be in?
Well that is if she ever returns to writing about the chaotic
world we live in.
However, the message did say something about being on
the search for inspiration
as she will continue looking for answers to her questions
which haunt her every night.

No poetry today;
she is still learning the difference between an exorcism
and break up.

The poet is closed today;
she wonders why her mother appears to be shocked at the
view of her skin being carved.

No poetry today;
the poet has lost complete control,
as the one thousand thoughts have congested her mind
causing sickening hallucinations.
She will be back, eventually.

DON'T FALL IN LOVE WITH A POET

If you're thinking about falling in love with a poet,
I am writing this for you.

I am writing this to save you from suffering the heartache
and woe.

Don't fall in love with a poet;
for their words they spill are carved from the sorrow found
within.
When the extravagant words they've finely sewn together
fall apart,
you'll discover the corpse of broken promises made by old
lovers.

Avoid falling in love with a poet;
as they'll have an urge to pick up a pen every time you're
angry,
comparing your eyes to the stars of the Galaxy.

With similes they'll teach you to love the flaws you deeply
despise,
as well as discover new things about yourself.

Don't fall for a poet;
if you're not capable of loving or comforting a walking burden.
Though if you choose to fall in love with a poet;
be sure to love them for who they are,
not the words they bleed.

LISTEN

Be sure to listen closely to their words for when they speak.

Even when they sit in silence, listen attentively.

CHAOTIC LOVE

For some reason I find it easier to breathe when I'm drowning within the chaos of your soul.

OUR LOVE

For every time you crossed my mind,
I planted a seed within the depths of my wounds.
Now I have grown a valley of radiant flowers of my love
for you.

PRICKLY THORNS

Though she was a rose
Scattered with prickly thorns he
Held her gracefully

AS SWEET AS HONEY

If only God could send me a lover that taste like the poetry
I wish I could write.

SAFE HAVEN

Allow me to explore the destination that will open your soul,

I will be sure to build our very own home.

VIOLENT STORMS

"Do you love me?" He asked.

She took a deep breath before replying:

"There are several violent storms within you and I've fallen in love with every one of them."

SURREAL

There is something familiar about you,
as if I've woken to your presence every morning my entire
life,
as if the constellations within your heart have always been
shining in my night sky.
You see this feeling is what makes everything so real.
We're destined for each other.

MY SHINING STAR

To others he was the sun;
near and harmful.

To me;
he was my only star,
glowing with radiance from a far distance.

RARE LOVE

She loathed how her skin allowed the lucid demons to
wander into the gaps of her broken bones. Every morning
they would intoxicate her hallow lungs with venom.
Triggering her to make irrational beliefs, that love is just
a rumor spoken from God himself, to laugh at us clueless
beings. Other times they would dance all night inside of
her mind as they chanted the names of those who have
neglected her. She was frantic with worry, refusing to keep
her eyes shut so she wouldn't have to face the dead for
when she fell into slumber.

Then he came along; evicting the demons from her body
as they couldn't bare the luminous light his eyes carried.
Mending every broken wound her body held with his
kisses, he filled her lungs with the scent of lavender. She
felt alive again as he granted her heart with an eternity of
love.

SEA SICK

His eyes were made of the world's deepest oceans,
with the specks of auburn scattered around.
On the sight of our first meeting,
I thought to have seen the galaxy within his eye sockets.
However I knew there was more to those precious
gems that went deep into his heart.
Anxiety danced throughout his body,
triggering his hands to tremble every time I spoke
about his eyes being so vast and full of life.
For when he cried the smallest part of my heart would
shatter as he had the tear drops sent by God from the
heavens above.
I could spend my days endlessly gazing into his ocean
as there is no such thing as being sea sick with him.

SAVIOR

Her head is lost at sea, full of sorrow and madness.
As she continues searching for the horizon's beam,
her lungs yearn for a hint of oxygen.
The only thing preventing her from drowning is the
soothing chimes of his voice,
calling out to her from shore.

ANTIDOTE & VENOM

You are the poisonous venom to my mind
& myself as a whole,
as well as the antidote to my broken scars & soul.

I'M WRITING MYSELF BACK IN

Since you left I've spent my days writing about each flaw
God had carved out to have created a walking masterpiece.
With your beaming smile, you warmed every part of my
body including the dilapidated veins I carried. I spent
countless of hours spilling ink on how your eyes were made
of sapphire, with the specks of emerald gems surrounding
it. From dawn to dusk, I explained how your heart
consumed all seasons of the year and boy did I fall for all
four of them. Till one day I unexpectedly finished writing
you out. I turned to the next clean page, suffering those
taunting minutes of writer's block. With a free hand I held
a pen as I began to write myself back in.

RARE DIAMOND

As the waves of the surging sea settled inside of my eyes,
you were there to caress and love me.
For when a sea storm of sorrow swallowed the rest of me,
you were there to keep me glee.
The fine chroma of mahogany you carry within those eyes,
consume the hidden pain and sacrifices you go through,
just to see other loved ones satisfied.
The bulging veins upon your calves are several ridges of
rivers,
flowing along the tract of your body.
From the depths of your elbows to the tips of your fingers;
carry the routes to the ocean inside of your chest.
I'll never be able to replace the years you have granted me,
to see me grow and succeed.
Or the unbearable pain you suffered bringing me into this
world,
but I will try to the best of my ability to bring you
coming years full of happiness and joy.

FATHER

The sacred scent of tobacco reminds me of your ubiquitous
presence you bring throughout my days of living.
For when I am surrounded by the ominous thunder of a
late night storm, I am reminded of the short tempered man
you are.
The immense tides within the deep blue sea symbolize the
hidden sorrow inside of those sapphire like eyes you have.
The thoughts which have deluged my mind, remind me of
the times you constantly challenged me to be strong and
independent.
The flakes which live on the surface of your skin glow with
radiance, just like the cratered moon God created to light
the night sky.
On cold mornings like today, the sun warms the bitter
heart I carry, reminding me of the comforting hugs you
rarely give.
Wherever I am for the; past, present or future, you'll
always be hidden in the heart of nature father.
I will always be home.

NEW FAMILY EDITIONS

She is a new born baby in the eyes of the world.
However to her mother, she is her very own universe.
She perceives the stars constellation within
her eyes and a meteor shower when she cries.
Just like Jupiter, a Great red spot of love imprinted on her
heart.
For when she smiles, it's a majestic vista of a shooting star
in slow motion.
Throughout the night she holds her securely in her arms,
just like the moon and sun of a full moon eclipse.
The feeling of every thought and touch she carries is like a
dancing
Aurora through her mother's nights.

FAMILY

The universe comes to mind for when I think about my
family.
Close together as we perform pirouettes in line after one
another.
My darling mother, the one who cares for us as
we continue revolving through the rays she shines.
Our majestic star, the sun, we praise the warmth of your
love you bath us in everyday.
My sister is Mercury as she is poisonous to us all,
cratered with hate and jealousy.
Do be cautious with the words you speak as
she'll erupt with anger unexpectedly.
My other sister is Venus as she is closest to our star;
covered in toxic clouds, though deep inside she is warm
and comforting with the glow that shines luminously.
My brother is planet earth as he is full of life with all
seven seas shifting within his chest.
Others nearby have the tendency of manipulating him,
yet he lives and strives boldly.
I am Mars, the coldest yet peppered with vast volcanoes.
With ridges flowing along the depths of my elbows to the
edge of my fingertips,
waiting patiently to spill the ink of my congested thoughts.
As for my father he is yet the largest planet among us.
He is high tempered with violent hurricanes gnawing his
soul.

Though with a Great Red Spot he carries,
there's more love and compassion he consumes to the core
of his heart.
My sister is Saturn, with icicle lashes and sharp edging
lips,
she is quite difficult to stop yourself from loving.
She is eternally secured as long as she is near our father.
For my youngest brother, the family's star,
igniting in the dark ends of our galaxy.
He might be the smallest, though he holds the unsaid
thoughts
hidden in the depths of our family.
We may drift apart in the years to come, however,
we'll always find each other within the heart of our
universe.

DREAM, REALITY, MEMORIES

At the very beginning you were my dream;
I desired to hear you say those three words that actors
said with such ease. I prayed for the day you'd tell me I
was your walking salvation. I only hoped for you to see
me in your night sky for every time you sat in solitude,
embracing god's celestial view of magic.

Unexpectedly, my fantasies turned into reality;
I began living my dreams with you. Everything I asked for
in my prayers, gradually played in front of me. We spent
our days laughing at each other's jokes, while we recited
each other's poetry. In times we felt empty, we held each
other tightly, just like the moon and sun during a full
moon eclipse. You filled in every gap my heart carried with
your love. Everything was just perfect.

*Until you walked right out of my life. I believe it didn't
happen overnight. I began losing pieces of you from the very
first time we met, till one day there was nothing left behind.*

Except those vivid memories. The images of your smile
haunt me in times I sit alone. Every time I recall an old
conversation, I feel a very small part of me shatter. I
recapture the times you would laugh and have a face full of
joy. Your eyes carried an immaculate spark for every time I
stared into your eyes.

However, the image has become a complete blur. It appears I have forgotten. What I remember about your eyes was when you said "we need to talk". Your eyes seemed to have been possessed because there was no spark to be seen.

INSIPID CUPS OF TEA

Among the dozen tea cups she had stored on the kitchen shelf, it was one she cherished the most. Every early morning for the past three years she had picked her favorite bag of green tea, pouring the exact amount every time.

Seating herself on the family's comfort chair, embracing the weather God had brought that day. After each sip she would analyze the floral design printed on the porcelain piece, tracing each flower with the tip of her index finger. She mesmerized the beauty of the Golden Lily White mug for hours as she held it close to her chest tightly.

This morning while preparing her cup of magic, she spilled it over. Falling to her knees she cursed and tried gathering the broken pieces. She stopped to stare at her hands that were now trembling with cuts and burns. She cried uncontrollably as she lost her breath. She could've cleaned the mess and boiled a new pot of tea, using another cup. Though she knew herself that it wouldn't taste the same.

M . M . S

You still exist in the deepest wounds I carry within my heart,
where you'll always belong.
Your name was the most significant yet the worst sound I
know till this day.

EVEN THE BEAUTIFUL THINGS FADE

The first time meeting she caught his attention,
he preferred her over the other daisies.
They spent their days hopelessly falling for each other,
keeping each other close on the windy days and cold nights.
It wasn't long till she seized into a moth-eating mess,
no longer thriving or beautiful. She was left dead & he
moved on.

SEASONS OF THE YEAR

He left her heart full of sorrow with a sickening twist
inside of her chest.
She tried her very best to heal her wounds he left with the
soil she once buried his goodbyes.
She watered them with her tears at times she could no
longer bear her nights of loneliness.
As the seasons of the year went by her scars began to
blossom with a bed of roses as though the seasons lived
within her pain.

NUISANCE

They say they'll mend your wounded scars while they're cutting deeper to the bone, baptizing your soul within the earth's dirt. They appear to use the hands you could sense in the years to come. The after taste of venom from the kisses they marked will remain on your lips. Their voice will be the piercing noise you will hear in times of being alone.

CAUTION: INK MAY BE PERMANENT

How she longed for those nights he once covered her arms
with his written poetry.
He was cautious for when he wrote over scars, made by old
lovers. He repetitively apologized for every time he thought
he was pressing too hard. She admired the way he curled
his lips while he read aloud his words. For the times he fell
asleep in her arms she smiled. Within the presence of his
warmth and security, she sighed in relief.

Months later, she spent her nights at war with herself.
Feeling the words he once printed, burning into her flesh.
As the ink courses its way through her bloodstream. It
is the venom she feels circulating through her veins. Her
heart could no longer bear the pain his presence caused.
Then and there she began to spill his poison from the tip of
her pen.

ON REPEAT

Our late night conversations ought to feel like adventures
with no destination.
Now they're filled with traumatic mental images of the day
you left me.

FOUR SIMPLE WORDS

I remember the time I wanted to ask the question that had
been burning at the back of my throat for so long. It was
four simple words I couldn't say without feeling frustrated.
I rehearsed it over a thousand times till it felt right. I
cried at some point because it felt so exhilarating reciting
the first two words, but the other two. The last two words
seemed to feel so heavy, unsure if it was the adrenaline or
the meaning that anchored my tongue to the earth's core.
I spent my days praying to god that these feelings flowed
both ways.

The day arrived and I stumbled over those poisoning four
words. You tried to cover your true feelings with a lie. But
you didn't, which I'm glad you did so. I'm relieved that I
can now live knowing the truth rather than die with the
unanswered question.

LIVE FOR THE THRILL

For the ones who have hurt you, it's inevitable to forget.
The aching pain is like waves crashing into shore, violent
and so unexpected. The memories that continuously haunt
you after midnight have found their way home, beneath
the surface of your skin. But it's important for you to live
on and make every day worth living.

You must forgive and let go of the past in order to move
forward. Set new goals, meet new people and make their
souls dance with happiness. Embrace every moment you
spend in the Suns warmth and be reflective like glass so
you can pass that light to others who are trapped in their
dark times.

To live you must take risks and continue dreaming
because deep within us all is a child craving for a late
night adventure they have not experienced.

HOPE

Hope is the revolting venom piercing through my flesh,
coursing its way through my veins.

It's what dilutes my rational thoughts and beliefs.
Making me believe that you'll be running back some time
soon.

But that won't be happening anytime soon.

OLD CONVERSATIONS

Our nights used to be filled with laughter and chatters.
The lasting conversations about our future together and
how much we loved each other.
Now they're lonely silent nights which are deafening.

SILENCE

She was the girl who had trouble expressing her feeling
with words.
She didn't communicate with sound,
though everything she needed to say was uttered through
her silence.

ADDICTION

He once injected his love through her veins, but now that he's gone it's the only this she craves.

DEMONS

After midnight is
when our demons
come out to remind us
of what we try our
hardest to *forget*.

MEMORIES OF US

The memories of us have found their way home and
it happens to be somewhere in the depths of my
hallow wounds. They seem to be absent for when I am
accompanied by other people. But in times of solitude, they
manage to travel to the right side of my ribs. Constantly
consuming the marrow of my battered bones, I sense this
sort of discomfort within my soul.

Eureka! They have discovered a despaired heart, with
edges as sharp as razor blades that would cut anyone near
to loving me. Piercing its sharp fangs into my heart, the
venom suddenly hugs my once bitter organ with warmth. I
must say it feels quite pleasant for a while, till the images
of your smile appear in front of me.

The hallucinations begin; I feel your hands intertwine with
mine as you press your lips against my cheek. I wonder if
I were to close my eyes and let the world carry on, rather
than write about it every time it occurs.

Possibly somehow I could awake to another day, where the
images are a complete blur and the sound of your voice no
longer hurts me.

WHITE LIES

Boy how I loved the stars constellation within your eyes,
not so much when your mouth was full of lies.

FORGETTING

"Forget me" He said.

She found it hard to comprehend as he slowly walked away.
Her mind pledged to forget the hands he used to caress her
with. However her heart felt the fingerprints he left upon
her ashen flesh.

Her soul chanted to eliminate the promises he once vowed.
But she could still see them written on the back of her
eyelids. The ghosts that stroll in her mind have planned to
erase the memory of his colored eyes. She cried for them to
not take the stars away from her night, as she fears to sit
alone in the dark.

An air of melancholy surrounded her as she could see
the silhouette of his body peeking through the darkness.
Seating herself in solitude she can hear him whispering
the untold secrets of his past. In a crowded room she
speaks with others nearby but she is somewhere else
with him.

She is told to forget the memories they shared together.
But she isn't yet ready to let go of him as his radiating
light has filled in every crevice of her bones.

THE NEXT TIME YOU'RE ASKED TO DEFINE LOVE

I pray for your blood to freeze,
while your mind sets to fire with
a thousand voices chanting at once.

I hope your skin begins to shred,
exposing the pallid flesh beneath with
your definition tattooed to the marrow of the bone.

I hope that your throat bleeds excessively as
you ferociously regret that
your heart howls *my* name.

HAIKU

She dwells on her past
as it seems to be the one
place she could love him.

UNTIED ANCHORS

He was an anchor she refused to let go of. Constantly grasping onto him as she was told there is no other love like his. Every time she told herself to let go, it was the riveting voices within her head which held her down into the depths of the sea.

Till one day she noticed her lungs yearning for the oxygen they once consumed, as they've been tarred with the murky water she wandered in. From there she knew he was the anchor dragging her down as she was an ocean buoy, longing to be free and alone.

She detached herself away from him, making her way to the surface of the water. Finally exposing her broken soul to the radiating warmth of the sun, inhaling the air her lungs desired the most. Observing her new surrounding as she embraced the pastel painting of God's masterpiece. She knew this was home.

STRANGERS & THEIR SECRETS

There's a bar out there somewhere in the world,
accompanied by lovers swaying in each other's arms to
their favorite tunes.
Spilling her secrets into his ears with his lips planted to
her neck.

Soon the day will come, where the music happens to be a
complete blare and the both have become strangers who
happen to know each other's secrets.

LIAR LIAR

He constantly drivels white lies from the edge of those deceitful lips. Trying his best to mask the truth with a smirk, though she knows it herself as the truth is dancing within the centre of his bulbous iris. Other broken promises and hidden secrets he keeps sacred, appear to be as transparent as the sun cloaking its self beneath the gray clouds of today.

OR NEVER

I wonder what you might think of when I cross your mind.
Which feature of mine evokes the mayhem within your
head? As you sit alone at night, do you hear me whispering
my fears & life ambitions into your ear? Do you ever
find yourself tracing the surface of your skin, where I've
written lines of poetry about your eyes being the universe?

Have you yet thought about your future and if I'm there.
Are we fleeing from country to country as we vowed to do
so? Have you seen those visions of us sitting on one of those
Parisian rooftops at night, talking about the times your
father doubted us.When you look up at the night sky, do
the stars constellation resonate your thoughts with images
of my eyes.

Maybe *someday* you'll be able to tell me the chaos
occurring within your beautiful mind.

MYTHS OF LOVE AT FIRST SIGHT

Please don't fall in love with her at first sight,
it won't impress her at all.
There is more to the lashes which shelter her
eyes that goes deep into her heart.
Spend a night with her beneath the celestial vista.
Here you'll find her heart blending between the stars
constellation.
The deeper you stare into her heart,
you'll find a bed of blossoming flowers watered by the tears
she once shed.
There are a few wilted flowers, destroyed by old lovers.
But she has tried her best to replace the soil and bring life
to what is dead.
Her heart carries all seven violent seas of the world.
Other times they could be settling with a gentle breeze.
This is her heart carving perfection out of the flaws she
despises.
So do fall in love with it or don't at all.

PERKS OF HOPE

I guess my mother chose to baptize my heart within hope,
in order for me to never give up. As a child it felt quite
adequate, if you ask me. Now that I've grown, it is as if my
heart had been thoroughly soaked in venom.

For the nights my phone would ring, I was praying it was
you on the other end. Waiting impatiently for me to answer
so you could beg for me to come back into your arms. But
you never called. Eventually one day my heart came to
terms of letting you go until it no longer hurt.

FOR THE 'WALKING TRAGEDIES'

For those of you who were known as the walking tragedy,
this is for you.
I am writing this because you skillfully masked a lot of the
sickening truth which had yourself at war every night.

I am writing it for all of those taunting anxiety attacks
where you felt helpless and alone.
I am writing this for all those hot days you suffered
wearing those thick sweaters, just to keep your scars out of
sight.

To all those meltdowns that have continuously went
unnoticed. For all those meals thrown down the sink just
to feel thin and empty. For all those nights you lied awake
calling for help as others slept in ignorance.

For those days you left home works unfinished or walked
out of class, and your teachers labeled it as "laziness".
Though it was a sign of how uninterested you had become.

I am writing for you because I was once in your state.
Crying out for help, no matter how loud I yelled, it was
nothing but white noise. I see what others don't, you're
hurting. I can't promise you that it will happen overnight.
But it will come to an end, eventually.

The tears you shed and he scars you bleed are not only valid but necessary because it makes you so much more of a being. You are not weak. These feelings don't define you as powerless. You deserve to get better and will recover from this nightmare because I believe in you.

You're just a wilted flower trapped in a late night storm. The morning sun will rise, so will you with such beauty and radiance. I promise.

SCHOOL TERROR

It's that time of the year,
as the school hall is crowded and silent.
I suppose I'm not the only one full of fear,
since the supervisors think themselves as tyrants.

I guess I've always been bad at test,
I seem to only succeed in writing about death and missing
old lovers.
My parents appear to be feeling distressed,
since their so called "Einstein" is no longer ranking higher
than others.

They must think it's easy living in constant anxiety,
having to put up with these high expectations,
placed upon me by our toxic society.
Death has become my recent temptation.

Distancing myself father away from my only friends,
just like the absence of oxygen within my bloodstream.
I've restricted myself to living in pretend,
constantly hoping it's just a bad dream.

But seating these dreadful exams,
I find myself struggling to breathe as my lungs feel as if
they're anchored to the earth.
My brain no longer functions messages to my diaphragm.
I have forgotten what I'm worth.

Maybe if our intelligence weren't defined by our grades,
I wouldn't be at war with myself.
Especially in my dark times turning to cold blades,
just to relieve oneself.

EMPTY STOMACH, A TONNE OF EMOTIONS

She only hopes to carry a stomach full of food without the bloating peeking. She hopes to live the next few days on an empty stomach, without her mother finding out. She hopes not to binge because feeling empty will only give her the glamorous thin look she wants for her dinner date.
Her skin refuses to take in the words of relatives she'd rather not hear like "you've lost too much weight" or "you haven't eaten enough" or "you don't look so well". She believes she looks rather ravishing.

Over the years she had tried to convince herself that food is an essential rather than a want. She feels as if the process is taking way too long but so was starving. She didn't wake up one morning restricting food for six consecutive days. It took months filled with fatigue days and nights with constant stomach orchestras.

On days like her birthday, she craved to have the pleasure of eating. Without having to feel guilty while she sleeps at night or making her way to the toilet, emptying her content.
She dreamt of living a life where exceeding her meaningless daily intake number without having to gain weight. Yet in reality she denies herself from consuming anything above ten calories.
Other times she continuously eats as if her hands are detached from her wrists, possessed by some demon.

She attempts to acknowledge the beauty of eating. She
is trying to accept the way her body looks without being
defined by a number placed on the glass scale. What most
of us don't understand is that she desires to be happy. But
not till she drops another fifteen.

She is troubled.
She is addicted.
She is dying.

Yet the nights she lies awake with an empty stomach.
She couldn't care less.

DAISY

She was just like a daisy;
In the full beam of light she thrived with life, swaying
against the wind currents. While in the shade she would
hideaway, drowning herself within misery. She allowed
others nearby to pick and crumble her into several
pieces, as they walked all over her. However she kept
herself silent.

On a summer afternoon, she blossomed graciously, though
her beauty was ignored by the others and herself. Not till
one day she is noticed by the unknown; gracefully picking
her up, admiring each and every flaw she held. She is
elegant. She is noticed. She is treasured for all of eternity.

VEIL OF DECEPTION

She was a flower within the farmer's garden,
blossoming with such beauty and delicacy.
Spending her days dancing to the whistling tunes of God,
blissfully swaying amongst the swarm of bees and
butterflies.
Other flowers nearby yearned for her company
while the others snickered with jealousy.
At the end of the day, the sun dipped itself within
the ocean as the others returned home.
There she stood alone, wilted against the damp soil,
looking above the celestial canvas of the night sky.
Longing to be placed among those glistening stars,
to perform nightly pirouettes around our pearlescent moon.

ON DAYS WE FORGET OUR WORTH

You stare down at the scale like you've done something wrong,
though the digits which appear will never outweigh the beauty held within your heart.
Ignore what the mirror speaks,
as it's only spilling lies to hurt you, don't let it win.
The stretch marks upon your thighs & stomach don't only signify the growth of us beings,
but they're milestones; reminding us of how far we've come in life.
So the next time you look into your reflection of the mirror, smile and tug yourself with the love you crave from someone else.
We seem to be neglecting ourselves these days,
though there is nothing more powerful and important than self-love.

HELPLESS TEEN IN NEED OF LOVE

On days like today,
I wish people around me knew without asking.
Praying for that one person who could somehow
sense that I'm not feeling well, not knowing the details.
On days like today, I find myself solemnly preaching my
death wish as I hope that the world could swallow my
whole
because my recent days have been quite chaotic.
It feels as if my hands are detached as they are constantly
shaking as anxiety dances within my body.
Days like today, my mother no longer responds to my calls
for help since I am known to her as the burden who only
craves for attention.
But that isn't it! I just want to be held in her arms because
sooner or later I might evaporate into thin air.
My day today wasn't so great so love me a little more than
usual since self-love doesn't seem to be enough.
My heart is melting into the earths dirt, I can not breathe.
So please, hold me in your arms tonight because no one
should be ignored for when they have lost themselves.

WASTELANDS

My heart is lost somewhere beyond these screaming
wastelands.
Days go by as it continues to howl with the wind, just for
someone to hear.
The rage of those late night blizzards have set it cold.
My veins no longer consume life as they've isolated
themselves from something so dark and bitter.
My heart refuses to speak another word.
It appears the silence speaks louder than the violent storm
it beats.

EXPELLING THE PAST

If water could expel the sorrow within me,
I would drown myself into a tsunami.
And if the darkness could erase the memories of you,
I will no longer need the sun or moon.
And if my poetry could excrete your love from my system,
I would write chapter books for months to get rid of you.
And if the wind could scare away my anxiety,
I will be outside mother, embracing tonight's storm.
And if my voice could teach the heavens to despise you
and to not feel such tenderness,
I will shout from the top of my lungs till my throat bleeds.

BLEEDING EDGES

Spending her days sharpening the broken edges of her heart, ignoring the bleeding cuts upon her hands as she attempts to put herself back together.

LATENIGHT WONDERS

She savors her moments of loneliness.
Especially on those restless nights she lives for
while others slumber in their ignorance.

I'M SORRY

I understand you despised how often I apologized but I
really had no other way of expressing myself. These words
filled with venom have found their way to the back of my
mind. For when I do remain silent, they course their way
to the tip of my tongue.

I'm sorry for the times I slept in and left my room untidy.
I'm sorry for replying instantly to your text. I'm sorry
for being that burden and I'm truly sorry about the fact I
apologize most of the time we spend together.

I'm sorry for leaving you unexpectedly since I was afraid of
being hurt, so I ran as far as possible.
I'm sorry for those times I cancelled on our plans because
I was too tired from the restless nights I was at war with
myself. I'm sorry for being there and asking if you were
okay.
What if the situation was different?

Probably if parents lowered their standards, they would've
took the time to return my god damn calls for help.
What if my sister spent her time reading my poetry and
understand what I'm going through rather than shutting
me out all the time. What if our society accepted me for
the person I have become? Maybe somehow I could be okay
with accepting myself as a being.

I'm sorry I can't control what my mind speaks as it appears to be quite occupied by the voices. I'm sorry I write too much poetry and I always spill my feelings out onto paper. I'm sorry for being the person I am. I'm sorry I have to brag on about those meltdowns and attacks that occur. I guess I should keep them to myself because you don't deserve to live them.

Do forgive me for wasting your time reading this, I guess I'm not so much of a great poet after all.

STRANGERS

The other day you questioned why the lady at the store purchased a shelf full of cat food. The community saw her as 'The Crazy Cat Lady'. Little did they know she was the widowed mother who had no cats, and cared for three little girls.

The girl at college who is known as 'the health freak', constantly staring at others while they indulged in their cravings. They said "she makes me feel uncomfortable". However, she envied the way others had no remorse while eating more than her daily intake.

You saw him as the old creepy man, who wouldn't stop smiling at you every morning at the bus stop. What you couldn't believe is that he once had a daughter of his own who had similar features you carried. She had the traits of a fine china doll. Yet took her own life because she wasn't "thin enough".

The boy in your class that's always happy and ranking high in exams appears to be living a rich, perfect life. What we don't see is the sorrow he masks very well every day. His mother is an alcoholic and his father no longer acknowledges his presence.

The new math teacher, the class constantly mock because of the way she's always fully clothed and flinches every time someone was too close. She lives her days in paranoia with mental images of that one night she was held against her will, sensing his hand covering her mouth as she screamed for help.

We walk past these people every day, millions of stories and thoughts hanging at the back of their throats, waiting to be told. Waiting for someone to ask. But it seems us humans are too ignorant and prefer to make sudden assumptions rather than hearing the hidden truth.

I FEAR DEATH

Friends of mine have always asked, "why don't you get much sleep?"

In response, I would silently curse the shadows beneath my eyes for exposing me.

My mother blames it on my fear of the dark and that I should stop overacting as it's all in my head. The truth is; there is no sight of darkness for when I close my eyes. Though mental images of that horrible night have been tattooed onto the back of my eyelids. Memories of you leaving me empty and heartbroken, continuously play on repeat.

As much as being alone at night, listening to my demons chatter terrifies me. Thinking about those deep brown eyes and mahogany cheekbones you carry, appear to bring me closer to death.

DEPRESSION

She is acting, though it isn't for a play.
Drowning herself within the sorrow and sadness,
watching others nearby breathe the surrounding air with
ease.
Her mind is lost somewhere upon these wastelands,
begging to be saved from isolation.
She continues to spend her days searching for a voice,
stolen by the demons hanging from the back of her throat.
Traces of sleepless nights, live beneath the rims of her
eyes.
She is constantly told to give up, yet somehow finds the
strength to carry on with life.

DOORMAT: WELCOME

She was known to be the human doormat;
spending her days waiting to be walked upon by others.
Why is it that she accepts this sort of treatment?
And why hasn't she yet moved?
Allowing them to tread their way in and out,
tattooing her bare flesh with their ignorance.
It appears as they see and feel an urge to use and neglect.
She must stop them and remember the sweet chimes her
heart once hymned.
She is to rise from beneath and dust herself, as she is no
doormat.
Though she is courageous and determined, and shall not
be stomped on.

ABANDONED SOULS

My mind is a city full of haunted ghosts.
No matter which road or alley I enter,
I seem to find myself facing the one person
I thought to have permanently bled out of my system.

ANXIETY

A lost breath within the lungs, constantly plaguing the inner walls of her veins. Scrawling thoughts tattooed in the back of her mind, remain unsaid. Another sleepless night with the doleful howls of her palpitating heart, calling for help. A serpent knotted in irritation beneath the surface of her skin, pleading to be released. The sharp bitter stares of strangers; driven deep into the depths of her livid flesh, exposing her inevitable insecurities. It isn't long till her soul is free as the words appear on the pages she binds.

SEVEN DEADLY SINS

The hostile world we live in today is infested with the
seven poisonous serpents, slithering amongst us. As
they are chained to one another, they'll do anything to
manipulate and anchor the successors.

There is Greed;
She longs for everything within her sight. Soaking
herself daily in the wealth and power God has granted.
Though truly believes her desires will see no end and that
anything the world has to offer will never be enough to
satisfy her needs.

For there is Gluttony;
Consuming more to fill his emptiness, since he is never
content. Spending his days overindulging in ignorance,
ignoring others who are starving and in need.

There is Envy;
Jealous of near success which she has failed. Viewing the
talent she lacks within nearby souls blossoming. Feeling
lonely and useless as the followers have so much more to
discover. Beware as she'll try anything to drag you down
with her sorrows and sadness.

For he is Lust;
He yearns for the flesh of other woman, not caring about
the taunting consequences. He craves for an unknown soul
to touch and love his rheumy skin; screaming to commit
the forbidden, just for the sensational

The falling sinner to Sloth;
Countless of days spent asleep within the dusky clouds
of Satan as apathy and sorrow are the only traits she
embraces. Others call it an illness or a state of mind,
however, they aren't the ones held in purgatory. She'll only
obey the evil melodies Lucifer speaks inside of her mind.

They call him Wrath;
He is filled with fierce hatred for those naive people living
highly. Constantly wishing death and torture upon those
who have hurt him or the close ones of his kind. He will
vent his anger upon others because of his own failures.

For she is Pride;
The one who can't restrain herself from staring into her
reflection for too long. Admiring the perfection she holds,
ignoring what is said by others as she only cares they're
chattering her name. Though the self-loving sin will only
appear when success is around, don't get too comfortable.

All seven sins cannot be seen, though all are waiting for
their next victim to destroy. Be sure to refrain yourself from
craving them or you'll be digging yourself six feet under.

MONSTER MEDIA

'Fresh & exclusive' is what they say,
as they continue to mold our minds day after day.
They continuously lack on what's truly occurring,
masking the truth with what other narcissist are
preferring.
Children of the righteous screaming,
now that their fathers have made the deceiving headlines;
"Terrorist have been executed" now streaming.
False accusations slithering their way through social
media
as everybody begins to follow like sheep,
ignoring the loss of innocence as another broken family
begins to weep.

HUMANITY IS DEAD

O lord,
if only you had given me the gift to scribe about humanity
and their rights in today's society. If only you could have
granted me the power to speak the minds of those broken
souls gone unheard. If only my words could articulate the
cries of those innocent children, whose fathers have been
killed. If only I could address my poems, to heal those
mothers being tortured and raped to keep their children
alive. If only I could express the agony of the innocent
children and find the cure to mend their broken hearts. If
only the ink I spill could rise against the media to spread
the truth and thoughts, that have gone unsaid.

OPRESSED WOMAN

If only you could see beyond the lashes of her eyes
and the headpiece wrapped around her head.
If only you could see her as a person,
rather than judging her appearance or mocking her thick
accent.
The silken headdress covering her hair doesn't
stop her from speaking her inner thoughts
or give anybody the right to call her "towel head" or
"terrorist".
Instead of assuming her beliefs; that she is forced and beaten
to lengthen the sleeves of her dress or to cover the flesh of
her legs.
Make the effort by asking her about her beliefs and morals.
Don't stare at her as if she's a walking mutant,
the both of you have blood circulating throughout your veins,
what makes you so different?
Stop making those biased judgments based on our
poisonous society's perspective,
the media is only looking for a good stir.
The hijab is not enforced upon her,
neither is it a choice only for him.
Her hijab is to conceal her beauty and praise her femininity.
She will never lower her tolerance for anyone or man to
mistreat her.

WHAT MAKES US SO DIIFERENT?

We both have beating hearts with blood coursing through
our veins.
So what makes us so dissimilar?
We both have no right to up hold any reins.
So why make people like me feel like an unwanted prisoner.

Does it make you any superior to me when putting me down.
Because I'm sure I won't retaliate.
Neither will I dare to frown.
Since I only respond to the ones who are taught to educate.

You try making me feel like an outcast.
Why? Because I'm known as the girl with the "towel".
Do know I will remain calm enough not to blast.
Since my parents, unlike yours taught me to refrain from
speaking foul.

So the next time you try putting me down.
Just remember I will not reply.
Only resulting you having a nervous break down.
So I dare you to give it a try.

MODESTY

As she walks upon these crowded streets;
she senses the frigid glares of the unknown,
burning into the cloth she wears.
With their fake smiles and subtle head nods,
they begin to worry if their lives are at risk.
Strangers continue to beat her with the word "oppress",
assuming that women like her
are suffocating beneath the veils they wear.
They utter offensive remarks,
thinking 'her kind' are uneducated
and don't understand the English language.
While nuns are acknowledged for their modesty and
devotion,
her people are seen as the walking terrorist.
Countries of the world have their own weapons and flags,
however her people are called the evil ones.
Islamophobia is gripping the necks of the innocent,
as they beg to be heard.

FIVE SENSES

You take a deep breath, absorbing the scent of tonight's
fresh air. Embracing the celestial view of the evening,
while the owls orchestrate the melodic tunes of their hoots.
Feeling the presence of your lover, held close to the right
side of your body. Silently admiring the exquisite taste of
their delicate kiss, marked on the surface of your tongue.

Meanwhile in the countries of war; the nostrils of broken
families are filled with gas, smothering them to death.
The screams of innocent children piercing into mid-air,
witnessing their father's headless corpse lay among the
scarred battlefields. Mothers are severely pained by the
wounds upon their gunshot stomachs. The people no longer
remember the taste of food, since the tears have stained
the roof of their mouths.

MEDIA ON WAR

"An Israeli soldier twisted his ankle in Gaza";
printed in black and white ink of the front page.
While thousands of the innocent Palestinians
are left killed or buried alive.
People in the other nations continue to follow like sheep,
blinded by the ignorance of the media.

They call it war;
though truly beneath these false headlines
are the screams and cries of the city children
witnessing their fathers being executed.
Tonight we will fall into slumber at was ease,
however over the oceans a mother fears
for the lives of her children,
as another jet is carefully planned to bomb the nearest
village.

Us Muslims stand for equality and unified;
yet we turn our backs because it isn't our
mothers being shot in the stomach
or siblings of our own searching for each other.
Whilst another son puts his toys away to search for his
father,
the others are digging the depth of his grave.

FAKE UP

Crimson cheeks, alluring lips with lashes as black as sin,
however she despised her natural state.
The mask she skilfully created was
worn for the purpose of feeling beautiful.
She admired the masterpiece which had concealed
the sleepless nights beneath her eyes and how the
eyeliner curved along her eyelid,
while she observed each and every lipstick
to cloak the exhaustion upon her lips.
Till one day she found herself vexing the morning routines
because she no longer wore it for pleasure.
Gradually she accepted and felt comfortable
within her own skin as she restrained herself from
worrying
 about the way her freckles scattered upon her
nose or the way her chin was structured.
Finally she had learnt to love herself for the true beauty
found within her appearance and mending heart.

PERFECTION PARADOX

An ideal type is not the definition of 'perfection'. Neither can it be defined as a state of attraction, nor perceived as a fault. It is a myth only seen in the eyes of hostile critics. A paradox made by the malevolent society we live in today. 'Perfect' is a contradiction constructed by the egoistical individuals, whom are truly blinded by their own desires. Perfection is not the size of one's body or the scars upon their arms. Perfection is not the state of mind or soul.

You see; perfection has no meaning as it's just another term, created to manipulate the perception of our own appearance.

DISTORTED REFLECTION

Into the realms of your mirror lies the dead corpses of
deception.
Joyously causing you to feel insecure,
continuously disfiguring the mind's perception.
When standing confidently within a gown,
the mirror will only begin to taunt.
Hoping to see you breakdown,
as their words alone cause to daunt.
You'll hopelessly fall for its lies
and you'll try to eliminate every 'imperfection'.
Weeks of dieting & exercising yet you remain the same
size,
within your eyes and the reflection.
Though the mirror itself carries such fatal flaws,
projecting its faults upon your face.
Blinding you with its dirt only because,
it envies the beauty you hold with grace.

WAR AND DRUGS

We live in a society, plagued by drug gangs and war.
Another clueless boy joining the crew ignoring the fact that
his family had strongly disagreed, for what they stood for.
He spends his days living in paranoia, for every time he
stepped out on the streets. It wasn't till then he was shot
dead, wrapped in pure white sheets. No phone calls to his
mother, as she is confronted from behind the television
screen. She chooses not to believe what her eyes had seen,
but it is her angel lying in blood of the crime scene. The
tone of her phone echoes within the surrounding air,
answering she hears on the other end is an unfamiliar
voice. It was the policemen officer speaking, as there was
no sign of rejoice. There she knew he no longer lived, that
her only child was taken by those foolish thugs. Living
their lives so carelessly, occupying themselves with deadly
weapons and drugs. She knew they were right about what
they had said. Once you're in, there's no way out. However
that is unless you're on a bed or lying six feet underground,
cold blooded and dead.

GRATITUDE

There was a time not so long ago,
where anger and hate ruled my lifeless body.
On every early morning,
I would soak my soul within the hope given by others,
praying for these riveting voices to disappear.
Now I see my days filled with happiness and awe.
The moon no longer witnesses my late night breakdowns,
as for now I peacefully rest in slumber.
My heart beats the chimes and words of gratitude,
to enlighten others living in chaos.
For now I know these days I am living,
is another wondrous gift from God.

MOON

I admire the pearly grin you flaunt upon the darkness of
our night,
as you listen to the wolves howl for your love and
watch the sea tides rise and fall to the rhythm of your light.
The sun may hear the sound of my canned laughter
& see the grinning smile throughout the day.
However you, my dearest moon,
witness the truth within my midnight sighs & silent cries.
ON THE NIGHTS YOU DISAPPEAR, I TELL MYSELF IT'S JUST
ANOTHER PHASE.
It isn't long till your presence returns into the stillness of
the night,
to accompany my loneliness as I speak my thoughts and
hidden secrets.

ODE TO MY OAK TREE

The way your crown sways to the tunes of god's whistles, have me whispering my untold secrets. As the sun beams with such radiance through your disfigured limbs, you guide me through the dark path I walk upon. The essence of your beauty has pervaded the air I breathe, filtering the tarred lungs I carry. Without you the forest is incomplete. Without you I am not complete, but neither are you. So hold me in tonight's storm as we listen to the soothing melodies your heart orchestrates.

DANDY DANDELION

We seem to underestimate the power of dandelions,
as they consume more than what we assume.
The whispers and dreams of the of the broken
are kept inside of each seedy cotton ball.
Everyday, new hopes and desires of the
despair are concealed within each blow.
Whether it be; a calling to the heavens above
or a wish to be lead through the burdens of life or a dream
to find true love.
This solitary ball of weed is kissed by the aspirations
of the young and the prayers of the elderly.
The feelings of longing, sorrow and loneliness
will soon be expelled into the air by fate.
So do keep an eye out for the next humble dandelion within
your garden.

LIGHT OF THE NIGHT

My saviour of the night;
illuminating the dark alleys
I hopelessly wander every night.
Searching for the signs of tranquillity,
as my heart can no longer
bare this afflicting pain.

LET THE WORLD WATCH YOU SHINE

The world will nightly watch your name ignite among the stars of our sullen sky. The celestial aurora will despise how you glimmer with such brilliance. The moon will sneer at your instant attraction you bring upon the ocean tides. Poseidon, the sea God, will speak malicious gossip as the sea creatures spread his words. Though you won't allow them to dimmer the luminous light you spark, as they enviously slither within the earth's dirt, speaking those lies.

Printed in the United States
By Bookmasters